ABSOLUTE BEGINNERS
Voice

T0057762

Written by Andrés Andrade
Project editor: Heather Campanelli
Layout: Len Vogler
Photography: Geoff Green
Models: Laura Odette Saenz and Brian Ogilvie
Music engraving: Len Vogler and WR Music Service

Recorded, mixed, and mastered by Len Hospidor
Female vocal: Laura Odette Saenz
Male vocal: Brian Ogilvie
Piano: David Pearl

ISBN 978-0-8256-3594-6

Copyright © 2008 by AMSCO PUBLICATIONS
International Copyright Secured All Rights Reserved

Visit Hal Leonard Online at
www.halleonard.com

Contact us:
Hal Leonard
7777 West Bluemound Road
Milwaukee, WI 53213
Email: info@halleonard.com

In Europe, contact:
Hal Leonard Europe Limited
42 Wigmore Street
Marylebone, London, W1U 2RN
Email: info@halleonardeurope.com

In Australia, contact:
Hal Leonard Australia Pty. Ltd.
4 Lentara Court
Cheltenham, Victoria, 3192 Australia
Email: info@halleonard.com.au

Table of Contents

Online Audio Track Listing 4

Introduction 5

The Parts of Your Instrument 6
Phonation, Resonators, Articulators 6

Before You Start to Sing 8
Stretching and relaxation exercises 8

Posture and Alignment 10
Standing Posture 10
Seated Posture 11

Exercises to Achieve Correct Posture 12
Rolling the Shoulders 12
Shaking Out the Arms 13
Carrying Bags 13

Breathing 14
How to Breathe Correctly 14
Breathing Exercise #1 14
Breathing Exercise #2 15
Breathing Exercise #3 16

Vowels and Consonants 17

Your First Vocal Exercises 18
Vocal Exercises 18
Warm-Up Exercises 18
Agility Exercises 19
Resonance Exercises 20

How to Practice—
An effective practice routine 21

Vocal Classification—
Soprano, Mezzo-Soprano, Tenor, Baritone,
or Bass? 22

About the Repertoire 23

"All Through the Night" 24

"Auld Lang Syne" 26

"Aura Lee" 28

"Beautiful Dreamer" 31

"Greensleeves" 34

"My Buddy" 36

"Scarborough Fair" 39

"They Didn't Believe Me" 42

"The Water Is Wide" 46

"You Made Me Love You" 48

Basic Music Notation 51
Reading Music 51
Notation of Pitch 51
Key Signatures 52
Notation of Rhythm 52
Note Values 52
Rests 53
Time Signature 54

Glossary of Musical Terms and Symbols 55

Vocal Troubleshooting 56

Online Audio Track Listing

Vocal Exercises	Female	Male	Backing
Vowel Sounds	Track 1	Track 2	Track 3
Warm-Up Exercise 1	Track 4	Track 5	Track 6
Warm-Up Exercise 2	Track 7	Track 8	Track 9
Warm-Up Exercise 3	Track 10	Track 11	Track 12
Warm-Up Exercise 4	Track 13	Track 14	Track 15
Agility Exercise 1	Track 16	Track 17	Track 18
Agility Exercise 2	Track 19	Track 20	Track 21
Agility Exercise 3	Track 22	Track 23	Track 24
Agility Exercise 4	Track 25	Track 26	Track 27
Agility Exercise 5	Track 28	Track 29	Track 30
Agility Exercise 6	Track 31	Track 32	Track 33
Agility Exercise 7	Track 34	Track 35	Track 36
Resonance Exercise 1	Track 37	Track 38	Track 39
Resonance Exercise 2	Track 40	Track 41	Track 42
Resonance Exercise 3	Track 43	Track 44	Track 45
Resonance Exercise 4	Track 46	Track 47	Track 48
Resonance Exercise 5	Track 49	Track 50	Track 51

Songs	Female	Male	Backing
All Through the Night	Track 1	Track 2	Track 3
Auld Lang Syne	Track 4	Track 5	Track 6
Aura Lee	Track 7	Track 8	Track 9
Beautiful Dreamer	Track 10	Track 11	Track 12
Greensleeves	Track 13	Track 14	Track 15
My Buddy	Track 16	Track 17	Track 18
Scarborough Fair	Track 19	Track 20	Track 21
They Didn't Believe Me	Track 22	Track 23	Track 24
The Water Is Wide	Track 25	Track 26	Track 27
You Made Me Love You	Track 28	Track 29	Track 30

Congratulations, you are about to sing! For many of you, simply picking up this book was a huge and courageous step. Something about singing seems to invoke fear like no other musical instrument—yes, we are discussing your voice as a *musical instrument*. Your voice, like any other musical instrument, produces pitches, rhythms, changes of tonal coloring, and dynamics. However, the human voice is the only instrument that can use words, facial expression, and even gestures to convey meaning and evoke an emotional response from listeners.

The study of singing is a process that constantly changes and the instrument is never completely the same from year to year, sometimes day to day. The instrument itself is the human body, and on any given day can be tired, stressed, joyful, sad, nervous, or in any other number of states that would never affect the performance of a piano or cello. The voice is always with its player, changes constantly, and is colored and enriched by our experiences, personalities, and by life itself.

This book is the perfect starting point for the beginning vocalist. You will explore the basic concepts behind a singer's craft, hopefully sparking an interest in further study. For a complete novice, the exercises and repertoire contained herein can prepare you to audition for a voice teacher in your area who can take you to the next step in your training. Perhaps you could sing in a church or community choir, a rock band or musical theater group, or just get together with friends for a sing-along. Maybe (and I hope you will) you can sing for one or more supportive friends who can give encouragement.

As you delve further into this book, it is important that you understand an important principle: A book is no substitute for an actual voice teacher. Probably more so than in any other musical training, vocal instruction is dependent on the ears and eyes of the voice teacher and that person's ability to communicate what are often very abstract ideas to the student. When I began teaching, I made it my mission to be constantly exploring ways to communicate concepts to an ever-changing student population at all levels of experience, and this is what I have attempted to do in this book.

There are many teachers all over the world, each with an individual point of view as to how the instrument works. Gifted teachers are those who are able to guide their students through practical exercises, sometimes imagery, and clear concepts that help a student discover how his or her individual instrument works. Hopefully, this is accomplished in an atmosphere that is supportive and encouraging, while still challenging, thus motivating the student to explore further development. If you do end up taking some lessons, ask yourself if you find the vocal exercises and repertoire comfortable. While it is important to give a private teacher a chance to help develop your technique (this may take a few weeks), you don't want to work with anyone who makes you uncomfortable, be it emotionally, psychologically, or physically.

So, whether you end up singing in Carnegie Hall or in your living room, I hope that this book leads to further understanding of this wonderful process, a deeper enjoyment of music and poetry, and many enjoyable times ahead.

Andrés Andrade

The Parts of Your Instrument

Phonation, Resonators, Articulators

Since we will be discussing your voice as a musical instrument, let's define the most basic parts of *any* musical instrument. All instruments, including your voice, are made up of three basic parts:

1. **Source of energy:** For singers, wind, and brass players, this would be the breath; for pianists and percussionists, the hands of the player.

2. **Source of tonal vibration:** For wind players, it may be a reed or the lips; for pianists, the strings inside the piano; for percussionists, the surface that is struck during playing.

3. **Source of resonance:** A hollow space where the tone resounds (on a very small scale, like an echo). For wind and brass instruments it is the tubing of the instrument; for pianists and percussionists, the inside space of the instrument.

For the singer, we can define further:

1. **Source of energy:** This will be the breath in the lungs, compressed and sent through the trachea and larynx.

2. **Source of tonal vibration:** When the above-mentioned breath speeds through the larynx, it sets up a vibration in the *vocal folds* (also known as *vocal cords*). We will use the term *phonation* to indicate sounds made by the human voice.

3. **Source of resonance:** The tone then resounds within the cavities of the head above the larynx, known as the *resonators*. This includes the pharynx, nasal sinuses, and the mouth.

In addition to the above three parts, the human voice (the only instrument to use words) also has parts known as *articulators*. These are the tongue, lips, teeth, and jaw.

I also like to use the term *secondary resonator*—the room or area in which you sing. We all love to sing in the shower, where we are usually surrounded by tile or hard surfaces on the walls, ceiling, and floors. Some rooms have a lot of resonance (echo) and some have little. This affects how a singer hears himself, and based on psychological factors, can make it easier or harder to sing. Because of this phenomenon, it is important for a singer to focus on *feeling* themselves sing, rather than *listening* to themselves. It helps to notice, but not be overly controlling of, the sensations of breathing, pronunciation, and some of the vibrations that you might feel.

As in any new venture, it helps to know the parts of the instrument as we refer to them in this book. Here are some terms you may encounter in your vocal studies:

Alveolar Ridge: The area just above the back of your upper front teeth (the front edge of the roof of your mouth).

Articulators: The parts of the instrument that help you pronounce words—the tongue, lips, teeth, and jaw.

Clavicles: Also known as the collarbones, they are attached to the shoulder blades.

Diaphragm: A sheet of muscle that acts as the "floor" of the rib cage. It is attached to the lowest ribs and its purpose is to pull air into the lungs. It sits like a dome that extends into the rib cage. During inhalation, it contracts (gets smaller), to draw air into the lungs. At this point a singer often feels an expansion of the lower abdomen. During exhalation, it expands upward into the rib cage cavity and the abdomen draws itself back inward.

Hard Palate: The anterior (front) portion of the roof of your mouth.

Larynx: A structure made of cartilage and small muscles at the upper end of the trachea that contains the vocal folds. The primary function of the larynx is to serve as a valve to prevent food and water from entering the respiratory system. When you swallow food or beverage and it "goes the wrong way," causing coughing and, more seriously, choking, it is because the food or beverage is making its way into the larynx. In singing, the function of the larynx is phonation.

Lungs: Sponge-like sacs found inside the rib cage that fill with air and are the principal organs of respiration (breathing).

Pharynx: The space inside your throat above the vocal folds in the larynx, extending up into the area directly behind the nose.

Resonators: The parts of the instrument where tonal vibration resounds. These can include the pharynx, sinuses, larynx, mouth, and trachea. The internal shape and size of each individual's resonators are what create each person's unique vocal tone.

Ribs: Twelve pairs of curved bones that protect your internal organs, forming a cage. The rib cage often feels like it is expanding during inhalation and contracting slightly during exhalation. As we work on posture, it helps to think of the rib cage as "floating," or held in a comfortably high position.

Sinuses: Small, hollow cavities behind the front of the face that act as resonators, opening into the pharynx.

Soft Palate: The posterior (back) portion of the roof of your mouth. Also known as the *velum*.

Sternum: The plate of bone where the ribs meet in the front of the rib cage.

Tongue: While you know what this is, it helps to understand that it is a rather complex mass of muscles attached to the jaw, as well as other parts, and extends down to the *hyoid bone,* from which the larynx hangs. A tense tongue can hinder both phonation and articulation of text.

Trachea: The tubing that extends from the bottom of the larynx, dividing into the bronchial tubes that lead to the lungs.

Uvula: The small extension of muscle that hangs from the middle of the soft palate in the back of your mouth. It is not directly involved in phonation, but can be a reference point for imagery during certain breathing exercises. Its purpose is to set off the gag reflex in case anything that is too large to swallow makes its way toward the esophagus.

Velum: The posterior portion of the roof of the mouth, also known as the soft palate.

Vocal Folds: Also known as *vocal cords.* The tiny muscles that vibrate as air passes through the larynx during phonation. We don't consciously manipulate them during singing. Pitch changes are effected by changes of length and thickness of the folds, initiated by thought impulses.

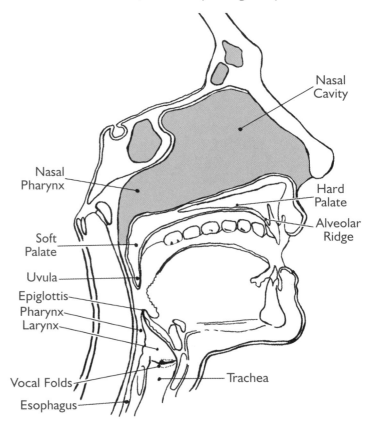

Parts of the vocal instrument: Head

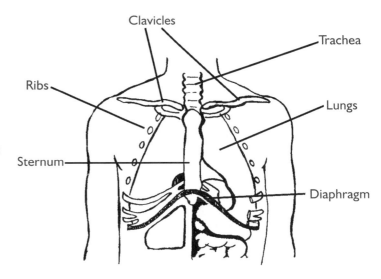

Parts of the vocal instrument: Chest

Before You Start to Sing

Stretching and Relaxation Exercises

Your posture not only affects your ability to get a good breath for singing, it can improve your appearance (look in the mirror) and create an air of greater confidence, which builds upon itself as you go along!

Before you start to sing, it is a good idea to practice this relaxation exercise to free the body of any tension along the back, shoulders, and neck.

IMPORTANT

If you have any history of lower back trouble, spine, head or neck injury and/or find these exercises uncomfortable, please STOP! This exercise is successful only if it allows the practitioner to locate tensions and GENTLY ease them out of the body by shaking or stretching.

Step 1: Stand up straight with your feet shoulder-width apart and your knees slightly bent (not locked).

Step 2: Gently shake the shoulders and upper body, then allow the upper body to drop forward as if you were aiming to touch your toes, allowing your head and arms to hang toward the floor.

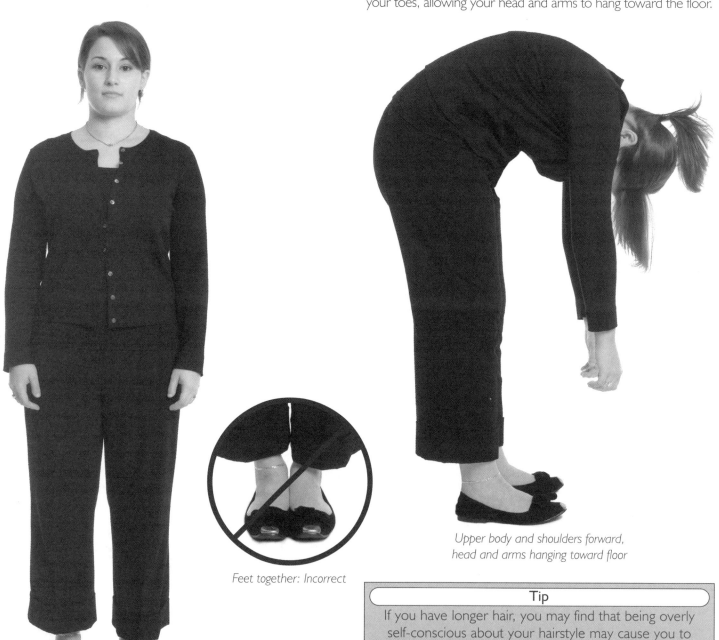

Feet together: Incorrect

Upper body and shoulders forward, head and arms hanging toward floor

Feet shoulder-width apart: Correct

Tip

If you have longer hair, you may find that being overly self-conscious about your hairstyle may cause you to hold your head with your face parallel to the floor, tightening the muscles in the back of the neck. This is the time to either put the hair up or not care about it getting a little messed up!

Step 3: Try to consciously relax the neck muscles and just let the head hang. Gently shake your neck and shoulders to relieve any lingering tension. Remain in this position a few seconds, breathing deeply. Notice the expansion in the lower back as you inhale.

Do not allow the face to be parallel to the floor, staring downward, as it involves using neck muscles to hold the head up. Just let the neck relax and your head hang as if the very top of your head were to be parallel to the floor. You will be facing your knees.

Step 4: Slowly begin to "roll up" to a standing position, visualizing each vertebra stacking upon the next in your spine as you return to a standing position.

Allow yourself a minimum of twenty seconds to return to the standing position. Leave the head hanging until the very end—it is the last part of the body to return to its place.

Head held by neck: Incorrect

Relaxation posture: Correct

Rolling up to standing posture, head hanging until very end

Step 5: You may want to roll your shoulders gently as your return to a standing position to loosen the upper back.

Step 6: In the final standing posture, the sternum is gently raised, the skull is balancing easily on the top of the spine, and the shoulders are neither pushed back nor slumped forward.

Rolling up to standing posture, rolling shoulders gently back

Final standing posture

Standing Posture

The relaxation exercise outlined on pages 8 and 9 is a great way to achieve the correct standing posture. First, let's look at a couple of examples of *incorrect* standing posture:

In this first example, notice the slumped shoulders and sunken chest. The collapsed rib cage will not allow for a proper breath and, with the ribs in this position, the effort needed to fill the lungs is much greater.

Incorrect posture: Slumped shoulders, sunken chest, collapsed rib cage

Notice that the subject's knees are locked and the shoulders are held too far back in a tense manner, causing an arched back. This posture, sometimes a result of trying to correct the former, will be uncomfortable after a relatively short time.

Incorrect posture: Tensed shoulders, arched back, locked knees

Now let's take a look at *correct* standing posture:

Notice the sternum is comfortably raised, one foot is slightly in front of the other, and the knees are not locked. In the diagram we see an imaginary line coming straight out of the top of the head—a good image to help you maintain this posture. The spine is curved normally and is in place to properly support the shoulders.

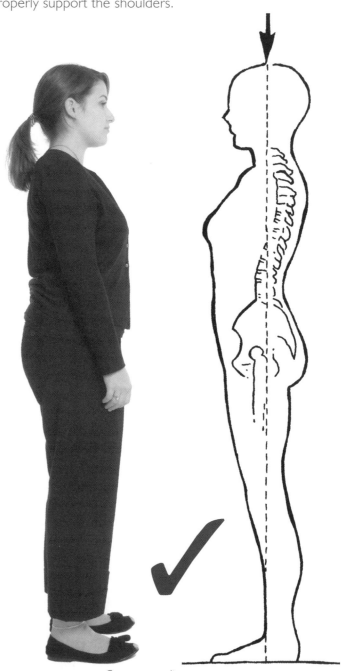

Correct standing posture

Helpful Hint
Imagine that you are a marionette and you have a string attached to the upper center of your sternum and another at the crown of your skull. With that image in mind, wiggle your head and rib cage gently. It should feel easy and buoyant.

Seated Posture

Though it is best to sing standing, you will sometimes be required to sing from a seated position during a long rehearsal, a choral rehearsal, or in some performance situations.

Again, let's first look at some examples of *incorrect* posture. Notice the slumped shoulders and caved-in chest:

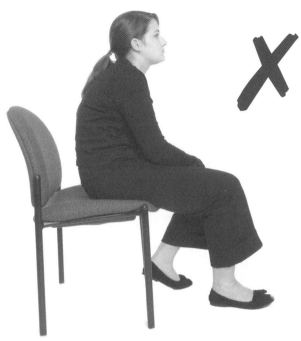

Incorrect: Slumped shoulders and caved-in chest

Here we see the singer is leaning forward with both elbows on the legs, holding the music like a magazine. This position can be quite fatiguing and does not allow the subject to take a full breath.

Incorrect: Leaning forward with elbows on legs just above knees, holding music in both hands like a magazine

In this final example of an incorrect sitting posture for singing, the rib cage is collapsed and it is now impossible to take a proper breath for singing.

Incorrect: Seated with upper back against back of chair, pelvis tilted forward, buttocks down to the end of the seat, sternum caved in

For a *correct* seated posture, it helps to sit somewhat forward on the chair, with your feet flat on the floor, as shown below. This way, the rib cage is raised and you can take a proper breath.

Correct: Sitting forward on chair, feet flat on floor

Rolling the Shoulders

After completing the stretching exercise, try rolling your shoulders, which promotes relaxation of the upper back and shoulders.

Then roll the shoulders separately, noting any tension that might exist there. Begin and end with the starting and final position below.

Starting and final position

Rolling shoulders together, step 1

Rolling shoulders together, step 2

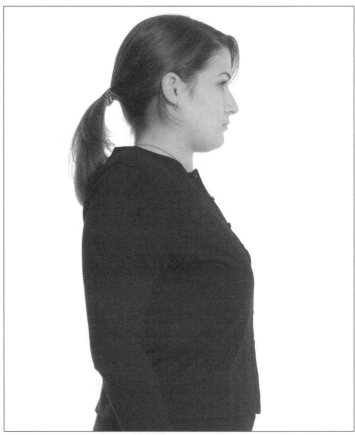

Rolling shoulders together, step 3

Shaking Out the Arms

Shake out the arms, beginning at the wrists…

…moving up to the forearms…

…then the entire arm…

…and finally gently twist back and forth, letting the arms hang loosely.

Carrying Bags

Carrying two equally weighted shopping bags (or buckets of water) in each hand is a good way to maintain posture. This exercise ensures proper placement of the shoulders.

Tip
Use a full-length mirror to practice these exercises. Remember, singing is a visual art as well as an audible one. A proper posture will not only make you sing better, but look better as well.

Breathing

How to Breathe Correctly

Sounds easy enough, no? The truth is, when it is done correctly, it is a rather simple process. Most babies breathe properly, and if you watch one while sleeping, take note of the easy, relaxed expansion of the lower abdomen, the area between the lowest ribs and the pelvis, including the belly in front. As we grow up, we are often taught to "hold our stomach in," either consciously or subconsciously in an effort to appear thinner or as an aspect of dance training (in ballet, one often hears the phrase "pull your navel in toward your spine").

When one breathes for singing, there is a relaxed, though not flaccid, state of tension in the diaphragm. When the lungs fill with air, they expand and bear down upon the diaphragm, which contracts and moves outward, causing a slight outward movement of the lower abdomen.

When the air is exhaled, the diaphragm expands and rises into the rib cage as the air leaves the lungs, causing a slight inward movement of the lower abdomen.

Mere awareness of this process can give the singer a point of reference to think back to when preparing to sing. The following exercises are designed to create awareness of the breathing mechanism while gradually building breath capacity. They can also be quite calming and mentally centering, not unlike meditation.

> ### Tip
> During any of these breathing exercises and while you are singing, it is important to keep the shoulders in a relaxed position, just sitting at the top of the rib cage. There should be no upward jerking of the shoulders as inhalation occurs. The shoulders should always remain in a relaxed state.

Breathing Exercise #1

After completing the preliminary stretching exercises, place one hand on your solar plexus (the area just below the sternum). Rapidly breathe in and out, in the manner of a panting dog. This exercise creates an awareness of the diaphragm muscle and produces a sense of relaxation, looseness, and flexibility in that area of the abdomen.

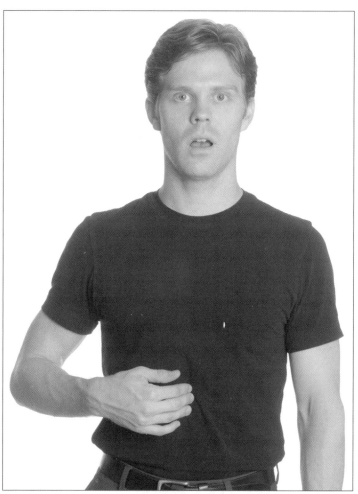

Panting with hand placed on solar plexus

CHECKPOINT

What you've achieved so far…
You can now:
- Think of your voice as a musical instrument (page 6)
- Name and locate the parts of your instrument (pages 6–7)
- Carry out stretching and relaxation exercises safely and effectively (pages 8–9)
- Achieve the correct position and alignment of the body to be able to sing comfortably (pages 10–13)

Breathing Exercise #2

Step 1: Take both hands and extend the fingers to make an "L" with the index finger and thumb of each hand (the right hand will be a backwards L). Place the hands with the inner edge of each "L" along the lowest rib.

Step 2: Inhale deeply, visualizing the breath being directed to those bottom ribs.

Step 3: Release the breath on an "s" sound like a hiss, allowing the rib cage and abdomen to remain expanded as long as is comfortably possible.

Step 4: Inhale again before you run out of breath completely. You never want to feel completely out of air. Repeat exercise.

⚠️ IMPORTANT

It is not unusual to experience dryness of the throat or lightheadedness the first few times you try this exercise. If this happens, please stop, relax, and drink some water if you wish. Return to the exercise after a minimum of ten minutes' rest. You will soon discover the extent to which this exercise is comfortable—do not try to force anything.

If you find this exercise easy and comfortable, you might want to try counting mentally while expelling the breath on the long hiss, first to twenty, then thirty, etc. This will build breath capacity and control the rate of expulsion. Try to make the breath last all the way.

This whole process should be easy and should not cause any tightening in the throat or torso.

Breathing

Breathing Exercise #3

Another helpful exercise is to lie flat on the floor and place a small stack of books (maybe two or three hardcover books or one large book) on the abdomen and inhale, noticing the lift of the books as the abdomen expands.

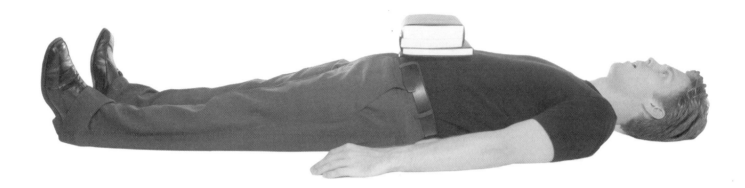

Floor exercise: Lifting of books during inhalation

Expel the air as slowly as possible on a hissing sound, counting mentally as the air is expelled. Do not allow any jerking motion to disturb the books.

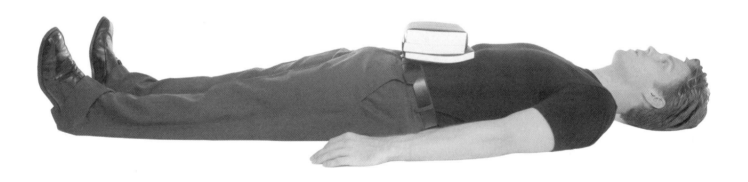

Floor exercise: Lowering of books during exhalation

Take notice of the expansion of the lower back at the bottom of the rib cage during this exercise.

Remember:
No two singers are alike, and while teachers like myself aim for principles that can apply to as many students as possible, it is important to remember that in the end, it must be a comfortable process.

Vowels and Consonants

Vowels

Vowels and consonants are the pathway and impetus for getting the voice out there. The next time you hear someone singing, either live or through media, notice that (with a few exceptions) pitches are held out during the vowel sounds of the musical text. While it is possible to sustain a tone while singing some consonants, most singing occurs on the *sounds* of vowels, which is when the mouth and throat are open and tone can flow forth without impediment.

Most vocal exercises are based on a basic set of vowel sounds, and more specifically, the open sounds most associated with Italian, Spanish, and other languages. (Many college voice majors begin their studies with Italian art songs.)

For purposes of clarity, I should differentiate between the names of vowels and the sounds associated with them. Below is a short list of vowel and consonant sounds that will be used in the vocal exercises on pages 18-20, alongside their corresponding *IPA* symbol.

The *International Phonetic Alphabet (IPA)* is a set of characters devised to help convey individual vowel and consonant sounds known to humankind across all languages. Some of these symbols are identical to our alphabet, but to clarify, I will always place IPA symbols between brackets [ ]. Here are the basic IPA symbols we will use:

[u]	as in "**boot**"
[o]	as in "alth**ough**"
[ɔ]	as in "**cough**"
[ɑ]	as in "**father**"
[ə]	as in "**gut**"
[ɛ]	as in "**bed**"
[e]	as in "**May**"
[i]	as in "**see**"
[ð]	*th* as in "**the**"
[ŋ]	*ng* as in "**sing**"

The vocal exercises in this book will use these symbols to indicate which vowels work well in each exercise. They are by no means the only vowels you should use but are a helpful start. You might find that some work better for you than others, and that is normal!

Consonants

While you may view consonants as letters that are not vowels, a singer, in general, uses consonants to propel vowels, making text clear. All of the vocal exercises in this book will have an initial consonant to propel you into the vowel sound. In singing, it is important to pronounce the words carefully, but one must not neglect to let the tone have its full duration on the *vowel*. For example, certain words ending in the letter "n" are often sung with the vowel closing on the "n" too soon. If I were to demonstrate in printed word, it might be:

- "green" should be sung "greeeeeeeeeeeeeeeeeen," not "greennnnnnnn"

Some other consonants that are often sung too quickly are "l," "m," and "r." It often helps to imagine that the final consonant of a word is "attached" to the beginning of the next word in the phrase.

This is but one example of many. A good singer will let the tone "ride the vowel," and put the consonant on "at the last second," but will do so with clarity. Some consonants that are easily allowed to become unclear are:

- The final "t" as in "boat"
- The final "d" as in "glad"
- The combination "nd" as in "hand"

The letter "r" in American English should be carefully guarded against creeping into a vowel too soon. It often helps to think of omitting the "r" and going straight into the next consonant, or thinking the word is spelled with the vowel plus an "h":

- Heart becomes "haht"
- Forget becomes "fuhget"

Listen carefully to several singers' handling of the letter "r" and you will notice examples like the ones above.

Like other parts of this book, this is an area that can be explored in much greater depth as your study progresses.

Your First Vocal Exercises

As you begin your first vocal exercises, remember that it is vital to maintain a proper posture throughout. It is important to take these exercises only as high or low as is comfortable on any given day, and never sing for more than twenty minutes without a break.

A few words about *glottal attack:* This is a type of attack that is produced when the vocal folds strike each other with a sort of "click" when attacking a vowel sound. It is best avoided at all costs as a beginner. Glottal attack can cause vocal tightness, fatigue, and other complications if overused. Pop singer Regina Spektor effectively uses glottal attack in some of her improvisational singing, but it should be used sparingly and only while you are under the guidance of a vocal teaching professional.

Note that in each exercise, I have listed various vowel and consonant/vowel combinations as options during vocalization. Each has its own benefits and potential challenges depending on the individual. As you become more confident, try mixing and matching the vowel sounds over all the exercises.

Vocal Exercises

We have included a male and female demonstration of every exercise. All exercises move in half steps—some move downward first, then upward; others move upward only. The best way to approach these exercises is to *listen* carefully to the demonstration before attempting it yourself. Listen to the vowel sounds and vocal tone, and notice how our vocalists only take a breath at the end of the phrase, while the pianist plays the next chord.

In the track following the demonstrations, you will have a chance to sing on your own to the piano backing. The pianist will play the notes of the exercise first, and then you start. This procedure will be repeated for each subsequent vowel. Please go only as high or low as is comfortable—it takes practice to extend your range so take it one small step at a time to avoid damaging your voice.

Tip

If you are a complete beginner, it is recommended that you refer to the *Absolute Beginners Voice First Vocal Exercises* pull-out chart included with this book. This chart will structure your vocal exercises for the first five weeks, slowly building up your confidence and strength, until you can revisit these pages and create your own practice routine.

Start on **Track 1** if you are female and **Track 2** if you are male, and listen to our vocalist sing the five vowels, one after the other. Listen to the pitch carefully and try to match it before attempting yourself in **Track 3**.

Warm-Up Exercises

These exercises are a great way to start off your practice sessions. In each exercise, keep phonation very smooth (*legato*), avoiding the sound of an "h" as you move through the notes of each exercise.

Try this series of five notes in a scale, ascending and descending:

Female	Male	Backing
Track 4	Track 5	Track 6

Next, try this chord, with pitches sung separately, ascending and descending.

Female	Male	Backing
Track 7	Track 8	Track 9

Let's move on to **Tracks 10–12**. Here we've added some syllables that help foster relaxation of the jaw. You should feel very supple as the jaw drops repeatedly. The jaw should be allowed to move freely during this exercise, but not unnaturally. Make sure you are getting a good breath before the phrase and keep the energy behind the breath moving through the phrase to the end. It may help to imagine singing a *crescendo* toward the end of each phrase.

Female Male Backing
Track 10 Track 11 Track 12

ya - ya - ya - ya - ya - ya - ya - ya - ya - ya - ya
bla - bla - bla - bla - bla - bla - bla - bla - bla - bla - bla

Now let's try some real words! The exercise below is great for practicing your enunciation. Remember to sing through the vowels and use the consonants to propel the phrase. Refer back to page 17 and remind yourself of the correct way to enunciate words while singing.

Female Male Backing
Track 13 Track 14 Track 15

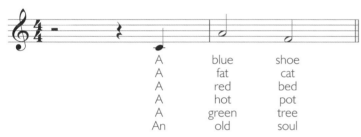

A	blue	shoe
A	fat	cat
A	red	bed
A	hot	pot
A	green	tree
An	old	soul

If your throat feels tight and constricted in the lower range while you are singing any of these exercises, it may help to think of "speaking" the pitches, sustaining the vowel as long as the rhythmic value of the note. If you are experiencing tension while singing in the upper range, sing through the passages on each of the five vowels to determine if one is more comfortable than the others. Then, modifying the exercise toward your favorite vowel, see if you can match the internal sensation to that vowel.

Tip

You might find that as you move upward in range, it is helpful to drop the jaw, increasing the mouth opening, to sing the top notes. Be aware of what you are doing physically when singing lower and higher. For example, do not move your head toward your chest as you go lower as that will impede the breath trying to come out of your throat and cause tension. Likewise, do not do raise your head when you sing high! Keep your head in the position as outlined in the Posture and Alignment chapter. Keep your throat open and relaxed, and be aware of tension anywhere in the body.

If you feel tense, revisit the stretching and relaxation exercises on page 8.

Agility Exercises

The following exercises will improve your movement between the upper and lower registers. Notice the slurs (⌢) and accent marks (>) in the exercise below. This means that you sing each group of two notes smoothly, with slightly more emphasis on the first (not too much, however). Listen to our vocalists demonstrate and you'll hear the result you should be aiming for.

Female Male Backing
Track 16 Track 17 Track 18

[zi_____ e_____]

Female Male Backing
Track 19 Track 20 Track 21

[zi_____ u_____]
[ze_____ o_____]
[ze_____ a_____]

Female Male Backing
Track 22 Track 23 Track 24

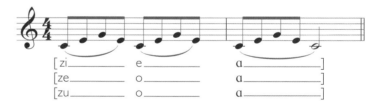

[zi_____ e_____ a_____]
[ze_____ o_____ a_____]
[zu_____ o_____ a_____]

After warming up, and going as high and as low as comfortably possible (without straining), move on to this wider exercise, which takes you higher in the vocal range:

Female Male Backing
Track 25 Track 26 Track 27

[zi_____ e_____]
[zi_____ a_____]
[ze_____ o_____]

If the voice feels strained and/or is going out of tune as the voice heads upward in the range, this can be a sign of singing too heavily in the lower voice and not allowing the voice to "flip" into the upper range. Drop your jaw and relax your throat. This will allow the voice to move freely into the upper range without having to strain.

Female Male Backing
Track 28 Track 29 Track 30

I see_____ you.

If you have trouble with the rolled "r" sound on "re-o-e," try speaking these words in the following manner:

* Pdessure (pressure)
* Pday (pray)
* Kdaft (craft)

Use the syllables "kda kda kda kda" on any of the vocal exercises in this book. With practice, you may be able to reach a fully rolled "r" sound.

Female Male Backing
Track 31 Track 32 Track 33

[ze - o - e - o - e - o - e - o - e]
[re - o - e - o - e - o - e - o - e]
[ze - a - e - a - e - a - e - a - e]

Female Male Backing
Track 34 Track 35 Track 36

[zi - u - i - u - i - u - i - u - i]

Resonance Exercises

Really try to feel the "buzz" of resonance in your nasal cavity when you sing through these exercises. When you hum ("m"), keep your teeth slightly apart behind closed lips, and jaw very relaxed.

Female Male Backing
Track 37 Track 38 Track 39

m_____
ming - ming - ming - ming - ming
[ne - ne - ne - ne - ne]
[ŋ_____]

Female Male Backing
Track 40 Track 41 Track 42

[re - no - ne - no - ne - no - ne - no - ne]

Female Male Backing
Track 43 Track 44 Track 45

lip trill_____

Female Male Backing
Track 46 Track 47 Track 48

rolled r_____

Keep the "d" in "du" soft—not too much attack.

Female Male Backing
Track 49 Track 50 Track 51

[zi - u - i - u - i - u - i - u - i]
[du - du - du - du - du - du - du - du - du]

An Effective Daily Routine

1. **Stretching:** Spend about five minutes stretching, while breathing deeply. Check your posture to assure a free, floating rib cage, and straight (not rigid) spine. Depending on individual habits, this may be practiced several times daily, without singing, to form correct posture habits.

2. **Breathing:** Place hands along the lower ribs and inhale through the mouth, mentally directing the air to your lower rib area. Notice the expansion. There should be no upward jerking of shoulders. Exhale on a hiss for as many counts as possible, but always have a bit of air left over in your lungs. Do not squeeze out your last bit of air. Continue these exercises for about five minutes.

3. **Warm Up the Voice:** Begin by gently singing through a few of the warm-up exercises on pages 18-19, or from your pull-out chart. Make sure you sing all the vowel sounds. Remember, only go as high or low as is comfortable on any given day.

4. **Go Into the Top Voice:** Start going into the top voice using long legato arpeggios. Limit these exercises to the most comfortable vowels at first, then work in the other vowels as you become more advanced. As a rule of thumb, the upper range requires more space in the pharynx (and mouth) than the middle range. The following vowel sounds are recommended:

    WOMEN: [u] - [ɔ] - [ɑ] - [i]
    MEN: [e] - [i] - [ə] - [ɔ]

    Not all voices will respond equally to these suggested vowels, so you must find the vowel that works best for you and adjust the others to match the quality and ease of the better vowels.

5. **Work on Agility:** Now that the voice is warmed up, try some slightly faster exercises like those on pages 19-20.

6. **Find the Resonance:** Exercises using "ŋ," and "m" are great for getting your resonators going.

As you progress, you may be able to lengthen the time you spend singing exercises between breaks. Do not sing for any period longer than twenty minutes without taking a break.

Remember:

Some days will be more difficult than others due to differing physical conditions, mood, amount of sleep, amount of talking done that day, stress, etc. On such days one should be kind to the voice by not insisting on extremes of range, dynamics, or flexibility. Between each of these exercise groups, allow a rest period of at least ten minutes. It often helps to spread these exercises out during the day, occasionally back-tracking to the former group of exercises as needed. A well-treated voice will always respond more dependably than one that has been muscled into submission.

Vocal Classification

Soprano, Mezzo-Soprano, Tenor, Baritone, or Bass?

While it is often difficult to accurately place a voice into any of these categories, these range guidelines will help you to explore new repertoire on your own.

Range reflects the total span of notes possible for a voice. *Tessitura* refers to the area on the musical staff where a voice is most comfortable spending an extended length of time.

Here are some very general attributes of range, tone, and tessitura, along with some famous examples of each:

Soprano (female and some prepubescent boys)
Range:

Examples: Renée Fleming, Shirley Jones, Audra McDonald, Minnie Riperton, Ruth Ann Swenson

Mezzo-Soprano (also known as alto–female and some prepubescent boys)
Range:

Examples: Anita Baker, Janet Baker, Karen Carpenter, Ella Fitzgerald, Denyce Graves, Marilyn Horne, Peggy Lee, Frederica von Stade

Belter (female)
Range:

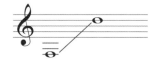

Examples: Patti LaBelle, Patti LuPone, Ethel Merman, Melba Moore, Barbra Streisand

Tenor (male)
Range:

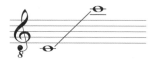

Examples: Plácido Domingo, Roland Hayes, Michael Jackson, George Michael, Luciano Pavarotti

Baritone (male)
Range: treble clef

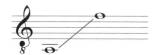

or bass clef

Examples: Rodney Gilfry, Nathan Gunn, Thomas Hampson, Gordon MacRae, Brian Stokes Mitchell

Bass (male)
Range: treble clef

or bass clef

Examples: Ezio Pinza, Paul Plishka, Paul Robeson

Hints on Choosing Repertoire

Now, after all your hard work, it's time to sing some songs! There are ten songs included in this book, suitable for both male and female singers. They are organized alphabetically rather than in order of difficulty, because with what one person may find "easy," another may struggle. This can be due to various factors including range constraints, or maybe the style of the song does not sit well with a particular voice.

For your very first song, try to pick one with a smaller range situated in the middle voice. If you feel uncomfortable or are straining to hit notes, please stop and either move on to another song or try an alternative key (see About the Online Material below).

When do I breathe?

Knowing when to breathe in a song is crucial to the performance. The most obvious places to breathe are when you see a rest in the music, and/or punctuation marks in the lyrics. I have also included breath marks (✔) within the music as a guide.

Try speaking the phrase out loud before you sing and notice when you would naturally take a breath if you were reciting the words as a poem. The ends of musical phrases are also good times to breathe—try to feel when the musical phrases begin and end.

Basic Music Notation

If you are new to reading music, you may want to read the chapter on music notation (pages 51-54). There is also a glossary of musical terms and symbols on page 55.

Songs

There are male and female demonstration and backing tracks for every song. The performances and backing tracks match the notation of the songs printed in this book.

About the Online Material

Not everyone will find the chosen keys comfortable, so with this in mind, we have made additional keys available online for download. Please note that due to the limitations of MIDI, there are no tempo changes within the online backing tracks.

If you have someone who can accompany you on the piano, we have also included downloadable sheet music files in the alternative keys.

Go to **www.learnasyouplay.com** to retrieve this material.

Ranges of the Repertoire

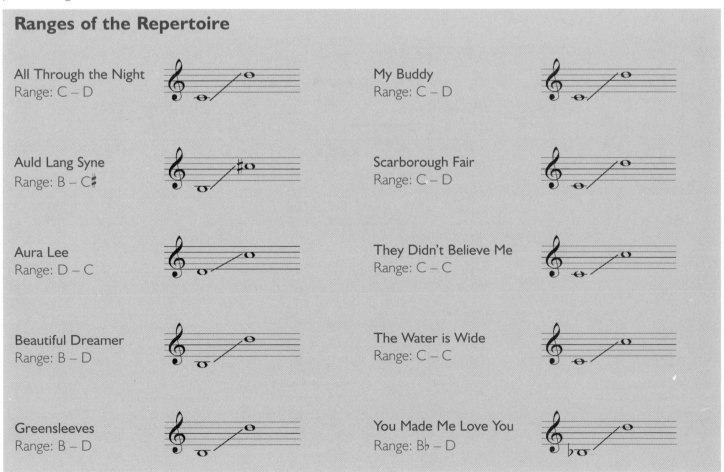

All Through the Night
Range: C – D

My Buddy
Range: C – D

Auld Lang Syne
Range: B – C♯

Scarborough Fair
Range: C – D

Aura Lee
Range: D – C

They Didn't Believe Me
Range: C – C

Beautiful Dreamer
Range: B – D

The Water is Wide
Range: C – C

Greensleeves
Range: B – D

You Made Me Love You
Range: B♭ – D

All Through the Night

Music: Traditional. Lyrics: Harry Boulton

This old Welsh lullaby dates back to the 18th century and is presented here in translation (the Welsh title is "Ar Hyd y Nos").

As a lullaby, it is to be sung with clear tone, in an easy production that still presents clean enunciation. The middle section ("Soft the drowsy hours are creeping...") can be sung with a broader approach, feeling the voice "sing out" as you ascend the scale.

In this, and other songs that present phrases that stretch upward, you can practice the melody without the text, singing on [du] or even using the words' vowels without the consonants. The latter might be tricky at first, but keep practicing and it will be worth the effort.

Auld Lang Syne

Traditional

Female
Track 4

Male
Track 5

Backing
Track 6

This traditional New Year's celebration song should be approached in an almost march-like manner. Try to physically feel the rhythmic pulse of this song before you try singing it—you could even try marching on the spot to get into the groove!

The pronunciation of consonants should be crisp and clear.

Keep the breath support low while singing "out" in this song, especially if you are a female who wants to try belting in this one (possibly in the lower key offered online.) You might also want to wait until after you've sung this song before you start drinking champagne, as the alcohol can be quite drying to the vocal folds—and don't forget to get plenty of rest and hydration the next day!

Aura Lee

Traditional

You may have heard this American Civil War–era melody in one of its later musical incarnations, "Love Me Tender," made popular by Elvis Presley.

Pay attention to the phrasing implied by the punctuation, pausing slightly at each comma and period, even if you do not take an extra breath (though you are certainly allowed to do so).

Also, give care to the intonation of descending intervals (e.g., "in the spring," "heard him," "along with," "take my"), as it is easy to neglect the lower pitches when approached from above.

Beautiful Dreamer

Stephen Foster

Stephen Foster was one of the first major American song composers to achieve worldwide fame.
He wrote many well-known songs, such as "Oh! Susanna" and "Camptown Races."

This song should be treated almost like a lullaby, sung in a clear, *legato* tone, connecting each note to the next, striving for quality of tone. Listen to how a violinist connects each tone he plays and you will get a good idea of the type of *legato* this song requires.

During the second verse, a slight overall *crescendo* is appropriate.

In both verses, make sure that the sound "t" is crisply produced, especially at the ends of words. In the same manner, the sounds "d" and "k" should also be crisply enunciated.

The word "dew" should be pronounced "dju" as opposed to "du," and all words beginning with "wh" should be sung with the "h" intact (e.g., while = hwail). This practice applies to all older songs in English and especially to classical styles (think: hwitch, hwere, hwy, hwen).

Greensleeves
Traditional

This song has a wide range so you may become very aware of the different registers, especially if you are female. Some male singers may also notice a slight change in sensation between the upper and lower portions of this song.

Aim for a "lilting" feel of two beats per measure, each divided into three (i.e., 1, 2, 3, 1, 2, 3 rather than 1, 2, 3, 4, 5, 6).

Make sure you take a good breath before the middle section ("Greensleeves was all my joy…"), and you might find it helpful to think a slight [u] (similar to the German umlaut "ü") while singing the [i] sound on top if it presents any difficulty. Allow each pitch to be clearly sung, keeping the consonants crisp, and paying close attention to the accidentals (multiple occurrences of C♯ and D♯ in the key of E minor).

My Buddy

Music: Walter Donaldson. Lyrics: Gus Kahn

This little vocal waltz was quite popular in the 1920s, later becoming one of the great American standards of the 20th century. Many influential artists, including Doris Day and Bobby Darin, have recorded versions of it.

As always, it is crucial to keep the tone sustained through the vowels, being careful to place emphasis on the first vowel sound in any of the diphthong combinations (e.g., stay on the [ɑ] sound of "Nights are long;" do not let it turn into "Naeets are long").

Keep a speech-like quality to the diction and bend the rhythmic patterns to match everyday speech (e.g., "Bud-dy" is more like ♪ ♩ rather than ♩ ♪). One way to achieve this is to practice speaking the text as a poem, finding the proper inflection of each syllable.

When in doubt, try inflecting the word on the wrong syllable to see how awkward it sounds, then aim for the correct inflection, allowing the musical rhythms to "bend" toward speech.

Upon the return to the beginning, you can let the voice part drop out, allowing for a piano interlude for the first page (re-entering at the phrase "Miss your voice..."). Alternatively, you can hum the first page during the second time through and resume singing the lyrics at the part mentioned above. This stylistic approach was popular with some vocalists of that era.

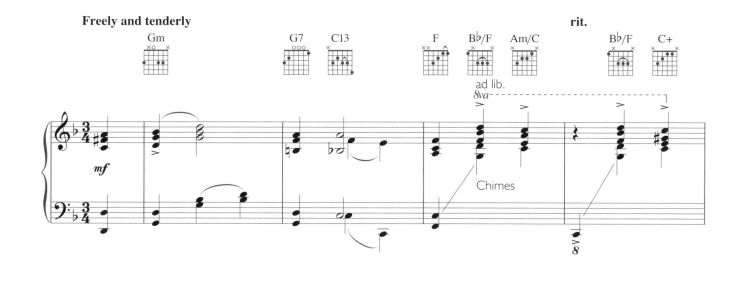

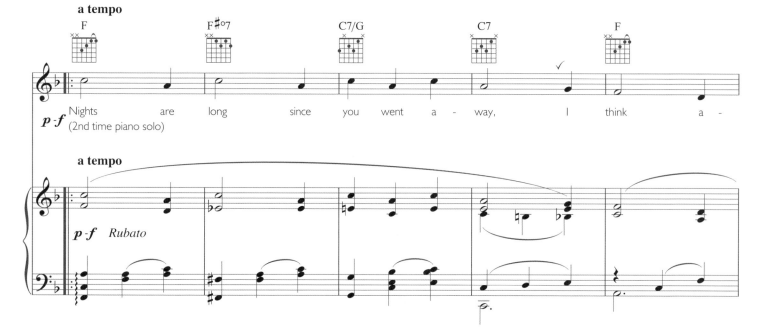

Scarborough Fair

Traditional

39

This is a very old traditional English folk ballad famously covered by Simon & Garfunkel
on their 1966 album *Parsley, Sage, Rosemary & Thyme.*

Folk songs such as this should be approached with a simplicity of tonal production that places emphasis on clear pronunciation of the text without undue pressure on consonants, and not neglecting good breath support. Female singers will find that a smooth head-voice quality is both desirable and appropriate in the middle section of the first page ("Parsley, sage, rosemary and thyme…").

Pay special attention to the accidentals (B♮ in our original key of D minor) to keep them in tune. When the melody is repeated with a different text, try to use a different inflection in the repeated phrase ("Parsley, sage, rosemary and thyme…"). You could almost treat this as an echoing refrain, calling one's memory back to a haunting remembrance.

They Didn't Believe Me

Music: Jerome Kern. Lyrics: Herbert Reynolds

> This song is from the 1914 Broadway show *The Girl From Utah*, and has been a popular standard ever since.
> It was even sung by Mario Lanza in his acting debut, *That Midnight Kiss*.

At the very outset, the word "and" must be sung with an extended initial vowel—avoid letting the "n" creep in too soon.

Treat the dotted eighth/sixteenth-note patterns (e.g., "beautiful you are…") caressingly and not too percussive in manner, almost implementing a slight *rallantando* into the next measure. In the phrases "Your lips, your eyes, your cheeks, your hair," etc., use a slight pause at each comma, even if you are not taking a breath. When singing, it is important to observe punctuation as if you were reciting poetry without the music.

On "You're the loveliest girl…" you can allow the voice to expand more broadly, treating "loveliest" almost like a quarter-note triplet rather than the quarter/dotted eighth/sixteenth rhythm as indicated.

E.g.,

love - li - est

When you arrive at the final note on the word "me," you can allow the tone to sustain all the way to the end, adding a slight *crescendo/diminuendo* if you wish.

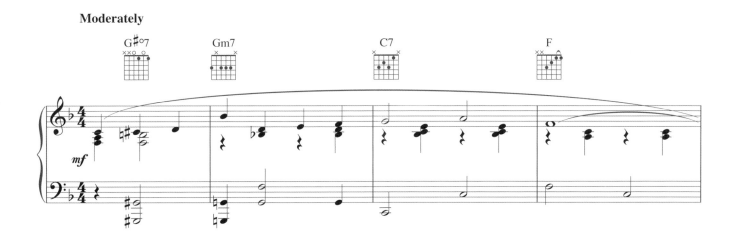

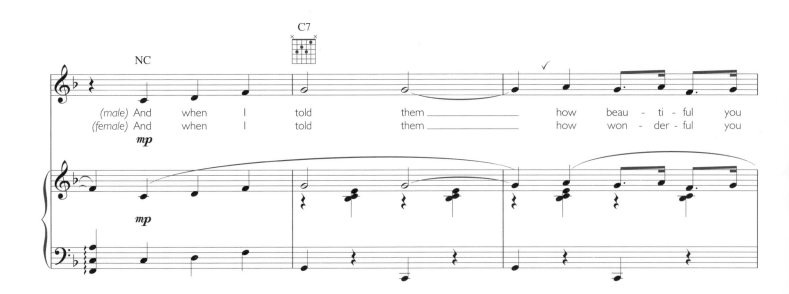

The Water Is Wide

Traditional

Female   Male   Backing
Track 25 Track 26 Track 27

Also known as "O Waly Waly," this English folk song has been around since the 1600s
and has seen much popularity over the centuries, right up to the present day.

Take a good breath before the beginning of each phrase, "spinning" the tone to the end, which may mean finding places to breathe where there is no punctuation. Pay close attention to the breath marks within the song, which should help you maintain a smooth phrase.

In songs like this that have a *strophic* structure (the same music for all verses), it is a good idea to "color" the text differently in each repetition of the melody to add interest. Read the lyrics first and try to imagine the story, if there is one, or try to interpret the words in your own creative way. Ask yourself "Why did this poet write these words?"

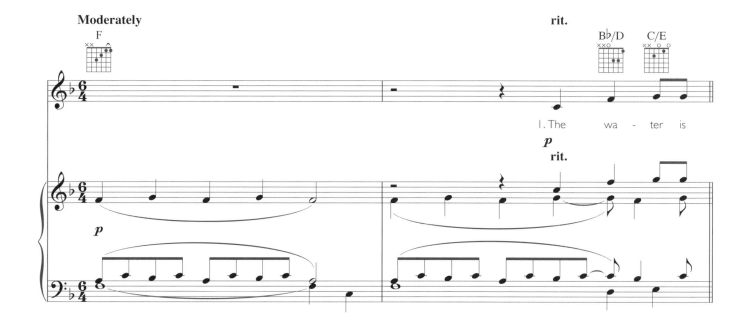

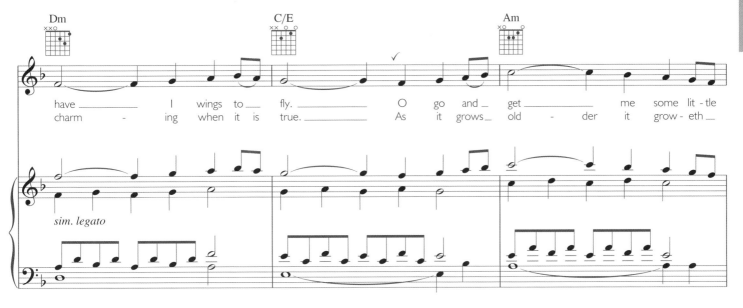

have _____ I wings to __ fly. _____ O go and __ get _____ me some lit -tle
charm - ing when it is true. _____ As it grows__ old - der it grow -eth __

boat _____ to car - ry o'er my true love and
cold - er and fades a - way like the morn - ing ____

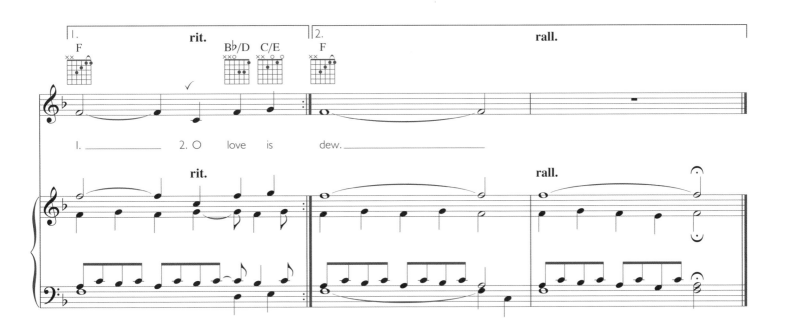

1. _____ 2. O love is dew. _____

You Made Me Love You

Music: James V. Monaco. Lyrics: Joe McCarthy

This song first appeared in the 1913 Broadway revue *The Honeymoon Express* and was recorded by Al Jolson that same year. It is often heard in the belting style, as made popular by Judy Garland in the film *Broadway Melody of 1938*.

Female belters will want to try the song in a different key (see online).

Keep the tone very forward and connected (*legato*) in the first phrase ("You made me love you"), and aim for a speech-like production in the lower pitches ("I didn't want to do it"). Relax the pronunciation of "didn't want to do it" by de-emphasizing the final consonants (the opposite to what one would do in more classical pieces).

Remember to observe the punctuation (commas) on the last page ("… love that's true, yes I do, 'deed I do, you know I do").

Male singers will want to observe the same musical approaches as listed above, but will not have the same challenges of crossing register breaks that female singers will encounter. Females may need to decide whether to belt this piece or sing it more legitimately. Either way is acceptable.

Reading Music

Although there have been many instances of famous singers who did not know how to read music, it cannot be denied that a basic knowledge of music notation can only be helpful in knowing how to turn the mysterious symbols on the page into actual music. Here follows an outline of the very basics of music notation.

Music is comprised of two basic elements, *pitch* and *rhythm*. *Harmony,* often referred to as the third, is comprised of two or more pitches and how they sound together, so we will leave that for another lesson. (Most humans can only sing one note at a time, anyway.) *Pitch* tells you how high or low a note is and *rhythm* tells you how long the note should last.

Notation of Pitch

Music is written on a group of five parallel lines known as the *staff.*

We must not only be aware of the lines, but also of the spaces between the lines. Any of the five lines and four spaces comprising the staff can be used to represent a pitch. The lines and spaces of the staff from bottom to top indicate successively higher pitches.

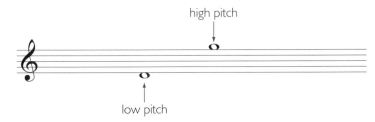

high pitch

low pitch

Ledger lines are used to extend the staff above and below its standard range of five lines.

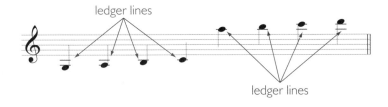

ledger lines

ledger lines

A *clef* is placed at the beginning (far left) of each staff to identify the letter name of a set of pitches. The *G clef,* or *treble clef*, identifies the second line of the staff as the note G. Notice that, when placed on the staff, the treble clef circles the second line from the bottom, marking it as a G.

The *musical alphabet* consists of the first seven consecutive letters of the alphabet: A-B-C-D-E-F-G.

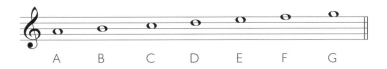

A   B   C   D   E   F   G

The notes on the five lines of the treble staff starting from the bottom are: E–G–B–D–F. Memorize one of the following phrases to help you remember these notes: "Every Good Boy Does Fine" or "Empty Garbage Before Dad Flips."

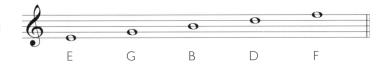

E   G   B   D   F

The spaces on the staff spell the word F–A–C–E. Remember this by saying, "In a space there is a *face.*"

F   A   C   E

When you add the lines and spaces of the staff together, starting from the bottom line, the sequence of notes is E–F–G–A–B–C–D–E–F.

E   F   G   A   B   C   D   E   F

A *scale* is a sequence of eight notes (the eighth being the same as the first, only higher) with a specific whole- and half-step pattern.

The *major scale* is comprised of two equal sequences of notes connected by a whole step:

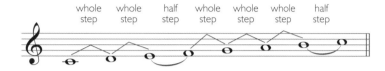

Accidentals are signs that either *raise* or *lower* a pitch by a half step and are placed on the staff immediately before the altered note. The three symbols used to notate accidentals are:

A *sharp* (♯) raises a pitch by one half step.

A *flat* (♭) lowers a pitch by one half step.

A *natural* (♮) cancels sharps and flats.

Key Signatures

The *key signature* tells us what *key* the piece is in. It is placed on the staff immediately after the clef sign and is notated by the use of sharps and flats.

For example, the key of G has one sharp, F♯. This means that every F throughout the piece will be played as F♯. The key of G is indicated in the key signature on the staff like this:

The key of F has one flat—B♭:

The key of C has no sharps and no flats:

Notation of Rhythm

The second basic element of music is *rhythm*. In the simplest of terms, rhythm is the determination of how long each sound is held. Rhythms for individual notes can be long or short, with extremes of each, and a *rhythmic pattern* is a sequence of notes played in succession with specific (regular or irregular) time values given to each note.

Rhythmic patterns are divided on the staff into units called *bars* or *measures*, which are separated by *barlines*. *Double* barlines show the end of a section, and *final* barlines mark the end of the song.

Note Values

Note values (duration) are determined by the notehead, stem, and flag:

A *whole note* (𝅝) equals four beats:

A *half note* (𝅗𝅥) equals two beats:

A *quarter note* (♩) equals one beat:

count: 1　　2　　3　　4

In order to save space, flagged notes like eighth notes and sixteenth notes are often joined together by a *beam*:

An *eighth note* (♪) equals one half of a beat:

count: 1　+　2　+　3　+　4　+

A *sixteenth note* (♬) equals one quarter of a beat:

count: 1 e + a 2 e + a 3 e + a 4 e + a

A *dot* after a note extends the note by half its value, so if a quarter (♩) note is *half* the value of a half note (♩), then a *dotted half note* (♩.) equals three beats:

$$\text{♩} + \text{♩} = \text{♩.}$$

Dotted notes can add a "jolty" feel to a song:

count:　1 e + a　2 e + a　3 e + a　4 e + a

Triplets are sets of three notes that are played in the time of two:

$$\overset{3}{\text{♪♪♪}} = \text{♪♪}$$

Quarter-note triplets look like this:

$$\overset{3}{\text{♩♩♩}} = \text{♩♩}$$

Rests

For every note value symbol in music representing durations of sound, there is a corresponding *rest*, representing silence.

For example, a quarter-note rest represents one beat of silence. A whole-note rest can represent one whole measure of silence, regardless of the time signature.

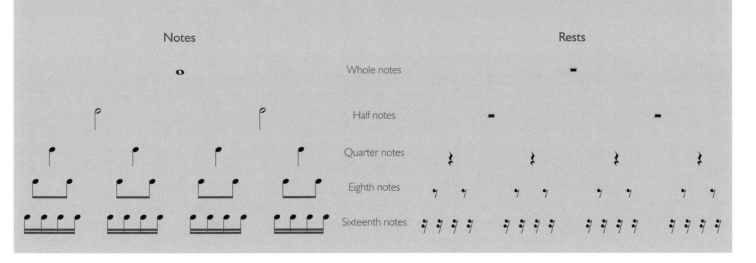

Time Signature

At the beginning of every piece of music, we find the *time signature* placed on the staff after the clef sign. The time signature consists of two numbers: the top represents the number of beats per measure and the bottom represents the type of note that counts as one beat.

The most common time signature is $\frac{4}{4}$. In $\frac{4}{4}$ there are four beats per measure and the quarter note is equal to one beat:

$\frac{4}{4}$ time is also called *common time*, represented with a time signature that looks like this: **C**.

Below are other time signatures you will need to know to sing the exercises and songs in this book.

$\frac{2}{4}$ time signature

$\frac{3}{4}$ time signature

$\frac{6}{4}$ time signature

In $\frac{6}{8}$ there are six beats per measure, and the eighth note is equal to one beat:

$\frac{6}{8}$ time signature

In $\frac{9}{8}$ there are nine beats per measure, and the eighth note is equal to one beat:

$\frac{9}{8}$ time signature

Sometimes you will see **¢**, which is "cut time," the same as a fast four. It just means it is easier to count two to a measure rather than four.

And finally...

Ties add the value of one note to the other. For example, a quarter note tied to a whole note is held for a total of five beats

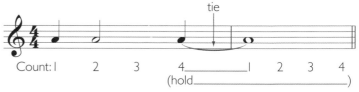

Structural Markings

These types of markings tell you how to navigate your way through the music.

|: :| Repeats

These indicate that a section of music is to be played again. Repeat signs appear at the beginning and end of the section to be repeated—unless the repeat goes back to the beginning of the song, then the beginning repeat is left out.

First and second endings

The first ending is played the first time through the section. After taking the first repeat and playing the repeated section, the second ending is played (skipping over the first ending).

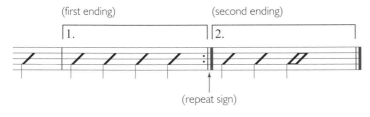

D.S. al Fine (or sometimes, D. %. al Fine)

D.S. stands for *Dal Segno*, which means "the sign." When you see this, go back to "the sign," (%), then play until you reach **Fine**.

Tempo Markings

These tell you at which speed to sing or play the music. Here are a few you may encounter:

Lento — Very slow
Adagio — Slow
Andante — At a walking pace
Moderato — Moderately
Allegro — Fast and lively
Vivace — Lively
Presto — Very fast

The following are indications in changes of tempo:

Rallentando (rall.) — Becoming gradually slower
Ritardando (ritard.) — Gradually slower
Ritenuto (rit.) — Held back
Accelerando (accel.) — Gradually faster
Più mosso — More movement, faster
A tempo — Resume normal speed after a deviation

 This sign is a *fermata* and means you pause on the note for a short while.

Dynamic Markings

Dynamics are very imporant—they tell you at what volume to perform the music.

$\boldsymbol{p}$ — *piano*, which means sing softly

$\boldsymbol{mp}$ — *mezzo-piano*, which means sing fairly softly

$\boldsymbol{mf}$ — *mezzo-forte*, which means sing fairly loudly

$\boldsymbol{f}$ — *forte*, which means sing loudly

You will often see the following symbols on the staff, informally called *hairpins*:

$<$

Crescendo (*cresc.*) means increase volume steadily

$>$

Diminuendo (*dim.*) means decrease volume steadily

poco a poco cresc. means "increase volume *little by little.*"

Expression Markings

Agitato — Agitated
Appassionato — Passionate
Cantabile — In a singing style
Con anima — With deep feeling and soul
Con fuoco — With fire
Con moto — With movement
Dolce — Sweetly
Dolente — Sadly
Doloroso — With sorrow
Espressivo — With expression
Facile — Easy
Giocoso — With humor
Largamente — Broadly
Legato — Smoothly
Maestoso — Grandly, majestically
Mezza voce — In a half voice
Parlando — In a speaking style
Pesante — Heavily
Rubato — In a flexible time
Scherzando — Playful
Soave — Gentle, smooth, sweet
Sotto voce — In an undertone
Staccato — Detached
Volante — Flying, swift, light

While it is impossible to give an exhaustive list of remedies to vocal problems one may encounter, below are some common issues that the beginning vocalist often experiences:

If you know and/or are told you are not carrying the tune:

Some students who cannot "carry a tune" find they can match tones consistently in a certain part of their vocal range, and can work to expand outward from that area. Combine this with the exercises given in this book to improve intonation.

You will find it helpful to familiarize yourself with the piano keyboard, which helps support the concept of music being an organized set of pitches, rhythms, and harmonies. This concept is sometimes lost on singers, who rely on tonal memory to play their instrument; that is, a singer hears a pitch or a phrase and reproduces what is heard.

If the throat feels tight and constricted while singing:

Try gently vocalizing with the tongue touching the lower teeth.

Work on relaxation by carrying out stretching exercises similar to the ones in this book. Some basic yoga stretches can also be helpful.

Revisit the breathing exercises in this book and become aware of your breathing patterns during singing, aiming to create a relaxed, open inhalation, followed immediately by an easy onset of tone. Think of inhalation and phonation as being one continual process, with no slight holding of breath between these two activities.

If the tone feels raspy and breathy:

Any of the following factors may be a cause, and behavior modification can correct the condition. Some factors that can inhibit vocalization include:

- Inadequate hydration
- Abuse of alcohol
- Smoking
- Excessive talking and yelling (especially in noisy environments)
- Singing for too long a length of time (more than twenty minutes without a break).
- Excessive caffeine intake
- Use of antihistamines, decongestants, and/or cold remedies that contain alcohol or menthol

Regarding cold remedies, try non-drying formulas, which thin mucus to a more comfortable consistency.

If you are starting a phrase in tune and ending out of tune:

Make sure you are getting a good breath before the phrase and keep that energy moving through the phrase to the end.

If you can't keep up with the tempo on the piano track:

Practice speaking the words in rhythm, with no pitch, and memorize the words.

If the tone seems "held in," the jaw tight, and words not clear:

Revisit the jaw relaxation exercises (tracks 10–12). You could also try singing the words with a slightly exaggerated (but relaxed) open mouth on the vowels, while maintaining crisp consonants.

Many singers record themselves singing and play it back to learn how to improve their own performances. At first this can be a bit off-putting, as most of us are surprised at how different we sound on a recording. Take a break and replay the recording several times to accustom yourself to hearing what others do, and then see if you can recall and connect the *sensations* of singing to what is heard on the recording.

If you find the upper tones hard to produce:

If you are a female singer, note that there may be what is known as a *register change* occurring anywhere between F and B♭ above middle C. At this point, it is normal for the voice to switch from a speech-like production to a *head voice*, which has a lighter quality often associated with softer singing, and folk and classical repertoire. Not what you would hear in heavy metal! Allowing the voice to "flip over" is crucial and resisting this change with too much force can often make the higher tones more difficult to produce.

In male singers, this change occurs closer to the top of the range, so men can sing a large amount of repertoire without having to negotiate this change. If the upper tones are difficult, try to make sure you are not singing with too much force or volume in the middle or lower part of the voice.

The repertoire in this book is to be sung with an easily produced, flowing tone. In voices of either gender, some songs may require a key change (known as *transposition*), and in certain cases, a different song altogether might feel better.

Other factors that may inhibit or affect vocalization:

Acid reflux, any illness or condition that robs you of energy, psychological or emotional upheaval, and physical injuries or trauma.

Refer to a voice professional if any of the above factors are not remedied by the advice given here.